HR MANTRA
INCREASE   EFFICIENCY

Prafulla Sharma

BlueRose ONE
Stories Matter

First Published March 2022

ISBN: 978-93-5611-223-0

BLUEROSE PUBLISHERS
www.bluerosepublishers.com
info@bluerosepublishers.com
+91 8882 898 898

Cover Design:
Shreya

Typographic Design:
Namrata Saini

Distributed by: BlueRose, Amazon, Flipkart

PREFACE

Indian manufacturing industry is a place where learning takes place every second for individuals at every level. In other words, to run day-to-day operations successfully, ideas, innovations and learning are the foundation for an individual to shape-up their career and take an active part in the growth of the industry. The contents of the book are the efforts to share the learning received while working in the different industries. This is an attempt to share knowledge, skills and ideas learned from blue and white-collar professionals in formal and informal interactions & through structured trainings, workshops, Projects (Aero Sapce AS 9100(Revision) C certification, Total Employee Involvement etc TEI). Every business unit be it professionally managed or family owned, require improvements in day-to-day work. This book flash light on how to improve management in a manufacturing unit by opting numerous operational tools narrated in this book.

The contents mentioned in the book specify techniques to improve organization's health and exercises to make improvements in manufacturing companies. 26 days' working, provide 52 or 78 opportunities (2 shifts or 3 shifts working) to all working individuals to learn and improve in line with the job requirements. The contents also provide insight on hiring techniques where a recruiter realize the sensitivity of hiring. If sales are declining on account of PPC, the contents share points on which PPC team can work to sustain and improvise. Adding further to the above, inappropriate appraisals attrition or unsafe working conditions in any unit lead to decline in belief of people in the existing function and if not addressed timely, it results in losing performers also. For any individual or company's growth, training plays a very important role, designing training needs, making plans, effectiveness are defined in the book. To judge and deploy a right person for the right job, designing job description, formation of key results areas and key performance indicators are important for the growth of the organization. Performance appraisal exercise has to be designed and implemented in line with the day-to-day business requirements to accomplish the effectiveness of working. Also when budgetary control alarms around with practicing human resource professionals, it is one of the effective tools to design and implement in way where results will be accepted as it involves people sharing. It also provides insights on employee retention of direct part producing employee attrition and steps to control techniques and helps in stabilizing turn around of human resource. Absenteeism is also an area for improvement where daily production hits if required manpower is not deployed. This book address tools for improvement in daily working by monitoring and controlling. When an individual works on these subjects, organization growth indicators show improvements.

For practicing human resource managers, in order to achieve desired results on account of people management and people development, insights on redesigning are mentioned in the book.

It is an attempt to realize efficiency, possibilities, results as individuals and aiming for continuous improvement and create a best place to work.

People Transformation - Role of Human Resource Lead

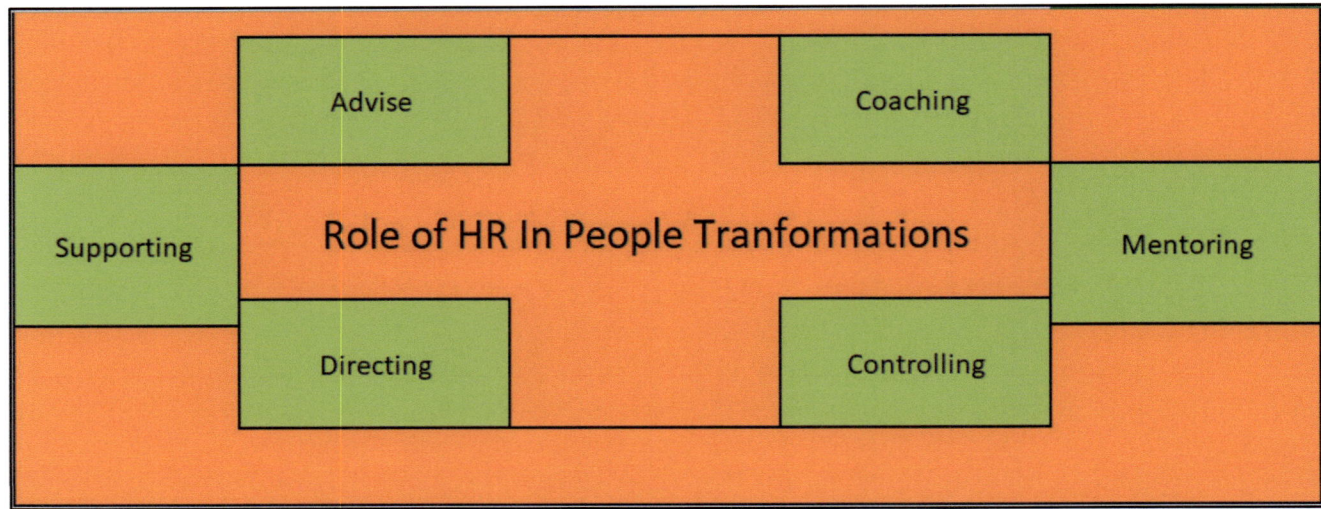

Human Resource is one of the key resource in any organization, for development and to achieve business targets. Machine, material, methods has limits to extend or upgrade but the only resource Human Resource which has unlimited capacity to upgrade and increases the effectiveness , inline to meet business objectives of any organization. Technical Team Members like production, Maintenance etc are the resource where their knowledge skills expertise is used in development of other three M (Machine, Material & Method). The next and most important resource human resource of any organization is being taken care by Human Resource leaders in organizations. Thus the ultimate aim or objective of human resource leaders is to observe, tap, develop and sustain good practices to create open environment of learning and sharing inline with achieving business objectives. Let us read how transformation of Human Resource is an aim of human Resource leaders and how they achieve it. There are various methods commonly practiced as training and development, classroom, on the job and of the job are well known methods to change, transform people in line with the departmental objectives. Apart from these methods suggestions, kaizen, 1's and 2's (initial stages of 5's) defects identification n reduction, air water oil, leakages control are other productivity tools. First step of people transformation starts with building trust, confidence by Human resource leader among team members through their uninterrupted quality services and hospitality. Second is design, demonstrate and sustain activities which has common interest of people around them and recognize best individuals periodically to enlarge environment of learning and sharing. Last but not least winning hearts and converting people performance in terms of increased suggestion, material identification and placing, good visual display and reduction in wastage creates environment of people transformation.

Managing People's Expectations

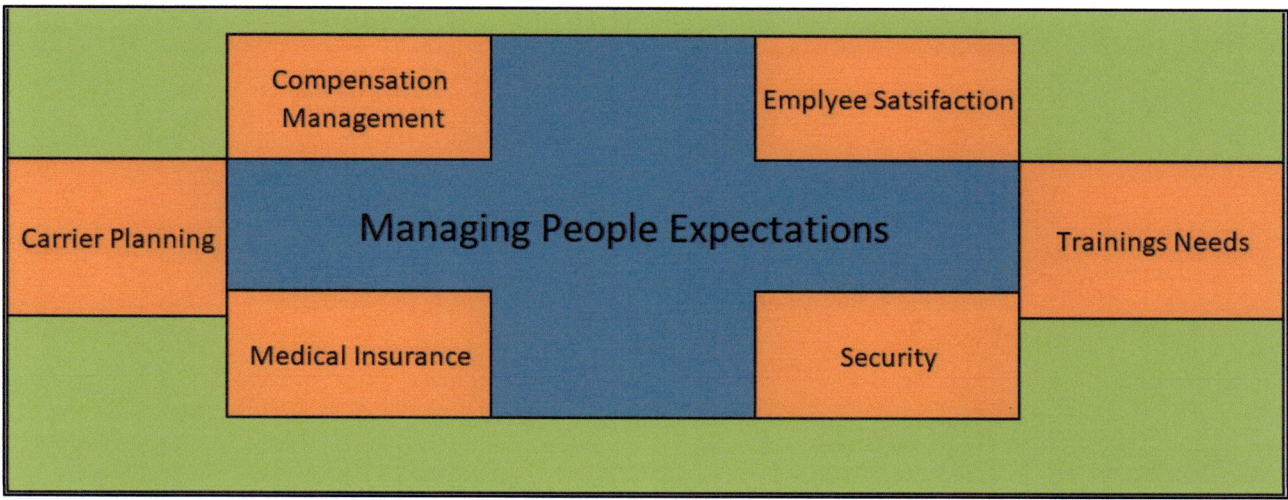

Understanding people's expectations is a very challenging job and managing it timely and precisely requires great efforts great thinking and require great personality. In industrial environment, people in forms of management representatives, government officials, employees at different level from diverse background together form a pool of expectations. In order to manage these expectations, leaders require great senses with them, in form of good listening skills, timely speaking, understanding people's thoughts, level, moods, anxiety, fear and other internal hidden personality traits. More or less managing different persons at same time requires dedication, doing best all the times, hard work, sincerity, patience, tolerance, empathy exhibits sound character of leaders. In today's tough times, where loyalty, courage and honesty are slightly declining from established standards, it is tough for human resource leaders to understand complex needs and changing behaviors of people around them. To manage people's expectations successfully all the time by the practicing leaders and emerging leaders with a focus on basic principle of human psyche, where love, sincerity and trust are top arrows in their bow to understand diverse human needs and its management with ease. Once again to conclude on the subject, managing people's expectations require clear vision and great personality of human leaders.

Contents

Chapter -1 - How to Select Best Employees

Objective-To recruit best talent in cost-effective manner within the time frame in line with the required skills sets.

Sr. No	Checkpoint	Objective	Marks
1	Education (MBA, B.E)	To match with the educational requirement to meet the job opening	5
2	Percentage-% of Academics)	To comprehend the academic record, Consistency or deviation in %	5
3	Total Experience	To comprehend experience (yrs) in line with the requirement	15
4	Stability	To comprehend number of years in each job to observe stability in each job and reasons for changes, also check for – 1-whether the candidate is leaving the job due to the performance failure 2-whether the job change is for unwanted hike .	20
5	Urgency to close job opening	1-Top Management's decision	5
		2-Strategic decision taken by Top Management	5
6	Communication & Presentation Skills	Ability to showcase the knowledge/skills with confidence and conviction	10

7	Aptitude	Ability to understand complex logical problems and their systematic solutions	10
8	Attitude	Behavior Pattern (Extrovert, Introvert), thinking, perception level	10
9	Personality Traits	1-Leadership Skills 2-Follower Skills	15
			100

Note: -Above mentioned criteria's are examples, these can be used as per specific hiring requirements or any specific hiring needs

Effective and efficient human resource functioning is an important function of any organization's growth, beside routine functions like time, office, salary & wages, administration, hiring. Hiring right person for the right job requires understanding regarding role, organization's values, culture and adaptability of potential shortlisted and final selection of the candidate.

This function starts with required job understanding, analysis and screening of short listing of best candidates. Next in line with the selection process is to match exact or similarity of profile in line with required skills, knowledge, similar industry and education level. In an interview, it is the combination of patience, knowledge and maturity for desired role to be taken in account in a perspective candidate.

A smart hiring professional draw a check sheet to fill information received during telephonic and face-to-face interview and compare the collected information with the set data of individuals with the job description of the vacant position.

For entry level, presentation skills, confidence level and appearance generally assure higher selection chances or we can say that these are desired and required selection criteria across the industries.

For middle level hiring, it is the job knowledge and stay with the previous assignments in line with budgetary are main concern areas for a recruiter.

For senior level hiring, similar industry, patience , temperament, maturity and role fitment are the prerequisite for any Sr level role. The check sheet in this chapter is designed to cater to major needs of a recruiter to select best fit for the required job.

Chapter -2 Designing Training Needs & Measuring Effectiveness

Objective- Improve and increase knowledge, skills to achieve business objectives

Sr. No	Steps	Objective	Indicator
1	TNI Originates from	Linkage with Organization, Department, Individual Objective	Effectiveness Measurement
A	TNI Form	Required for 1-Internal HR Audit 2-TS Audit 3-Customer Audit 4-Annual Training Plan	Number of employees
B	Competency Measurement Charts	1-To measure required Competency Level 2-To select employees based on the result of competency mapping 3-To select Best Performer on the basis of present level 4- Required for TS Audit	Target Competency Level Vs Available Competency Level
C	Skill Matrix Measurement Charts	1-Required for calculating the type of skills required for enhancing the required skill set 2-Required for skill assessment 3-Required to tap potential operators required for next level 4-Required for TS Audit.	Target Skill Level Vs Available Skill Level

D	Annual Appraisal (Etc-Functional. Behavioral)	1-Required to reward performers by way of promotion, pay hikes etc 2-Required for Assessing Performance of individuals throughout the year.	1-Number of employees Covered wrt employees required for appraisals 2-Number of Grievances' reduction wrt last year's grievances
E	Audit Non-Conformance	Direct communication by Customer to improve particular function, process , sub-process etc., wrt specified process, function, process, sub-process	Closing of Non-Conformance within time with mistake proofing if possible
F	Strategic Initiative	Training requirements by Top Management/CFT /CEO	Completion of project(s) decided by management after imparting training
G	New Product Introduction	Required to upgrade existing product to understand new product specification and convert the knowledge attained by producing pilot batch production	Time Taken against Target Time for producing pilot batch production
Compilation of TNI & Measuring Effectiveness			
2	Preparation of Annual Calendar	1-Part of Annual People Development Function 2-Required to understand total no of technical, behavioral, system training sessions planned for FY.	1-Number of Training sessions planned Vs Actual Training sessions Conducted 2-% of Objective achieved 3-Number of In-house Trainers Developed 4-Budget Control
3	2-% of Objective achieved	1-Part of Monthly People Development Function 2-Required to understand total no of technical, behavioral, system training planned for the Month	1-Number of Training sessions planned Vs Actual Training sessions Conducted,
4	3-Number of In-house Trainer Developed	1-Required for Daily Work Monitoring 2-Required for measuring Training Effectiveness	1-Written Test 2-Reduction in number of mistakes while calculating OEE after Certain period of training 3-Timly and accurately OEE data presented to management by trained individuals 4-Involvement by individuals in improvement activities 5-Increase in TEI

4

Chapter 3-Method to Determine Training Effectiveness – Returns on Investment (ROI)

Objective-Compare investment on learnings against (Target)objectives

Sr. No	Input	Output
1	Objective of training programmer to be defined (Awareness, Expert level, 1-Expert Level 2-Refresher Course	1-Number of errors to be reduced (Data Filling, Part checking Etc.)
2	Total time Required to complete the session (Eg.30 Min for on-the-job training or 2 Hours for class room training)	2-Up gradation of Supervisors (Reducing error in Shift Handling, Rejection Control, Etc.)
3	Break-up of Total time (eg. A-2 Min Introduction, B-5 Min Objective, C-30-40 Min Course Details, D-10 Min reinforcement, E-10 Minimum -Question Answer or Written Test = (60-70 Min)	3-Less Rejection Part Produced (Check Operators Performance at regular interval preferably once in a Month)
4	Observations of participants after attending learning session to be recorded	4-Less time taking by Operators for Same Job.
5	Feedback of participants to be recorded	5-Helps in designing better course or may be better faculty for the same training.

6	Written test of participants (To ensure learnings implicit by the participants and retained in conscious and subconscious mind & clearly exhibit during the performance)	6.1- Any Improvement in Productivity, Quality, Cost, Delivery, Safety, Increasing Morale (PQCDSM) 6.2 Pre & Post Test Evaluation (Marks or Score)
7	Report by participants for full day course	7.1 Report based on Effectiveness Criteria Examples 1-1S and 2S improvement plan after 5S audit 2-Revised PFMEA Report 3-Setpwise and stage wise Rejection / Reduction plan report

Chapter 4 - Developing Supervisor

Objective-To Develop second line of competent and skilled team members to adhere the schedule and improve manufacturing practices and final product.

Benefits of Developing Supervisors

1-Skill Identification (Desired Vs Actual)

2-Skill Development (Through on the job and class room training)

3-Increasing Productivity (PQCDSM Approach)

Steps of Implementation

1-Identify Supervisor's level on different required skill sets

2-Motivate Supervisor to upgrade skills by consistent training

3-Support Supervisor to understand the gap in skill(s) and improvise by practice

4-Reward best Supervisor, display picture of best Supervisor of the month at prominent place

5-Overall improvise production, quality, and supply

6-Healthy competition amongst employees

7- Constitute cross functional teams (CFT) to assess and analyze quality of data to understand issues in depth and provide corrective actions.

Approach of Assessment

Sr. No	Criteria	Unit of Measurement
1	Scheduled Production Vs Actual production.	Number / Unit
2	Quality Rejections	% of Rejection
3	Tooling Management	Condition & availability of tools against inventory
4	Machine Conditions	Number of Break Down(s)
5	Changeover Management	No of hours taken for changeover
6	Attrition control of Contract Workman	% of attrition
7	No of Implemented Kaizens	No of Kaizens
8	1S & 2S audit score	Score of 1S & 2S audit
9	Training & Development	No of hours of training provided
10	Attendance	% of attendance during the month
11	General Behavior & Attitude	Very Good (95%), Good (75%), Satisfactory (50%)

Approach of Development

1- Summary of Skill Assessment Sheet - Department wise

2- Training, Counseling, and Mentoring Plan for Supervisors Development.

2. A - On the job training plan - Department wise

2. B - Annual Training plan for Supervisor Development.

Chapter 5 - Awareness on Key Result Area (KRA's) & Key Performance Indicators (KPI's)

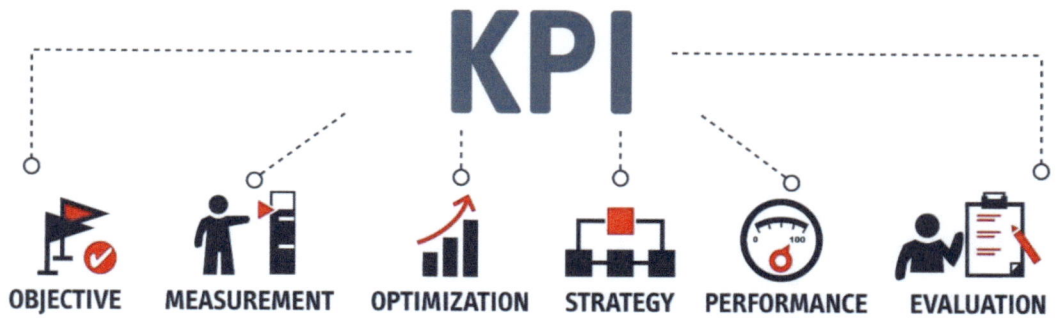

Objective-To develop understanding of Performance & Deliverable and compare results against set targets

KRA originates from Following

Organization's Vision

Organization's Mission

Organization's Objective

Department's Functions/KRA

Principle of setting Key Result Area

- Specific

- Measurable

- Achievable

- Relevant

- Time bound

KRA Setting Process

Organization's Objective

Department's Objective

Individual's Objective

SAMPLE - KRA Score Card

Sr. No.	KRA	Target	UOM	April-21	May-21	June-21	July-21	Aug-21	Sept-21
1	Increase Training man days	2H/PE/PM	Hours	2	2	1	2	2	2
2	KRA Implementation	100%	Nos	75	80	15	90	90	95
3	Improvement in 1S & 2S	75%	%	50	60	10	75	75	75
4	Employee Participation (Suggestion Schemes / Kaizen)	2/PE/PM	%	.5	.6	.7	.8	.9	1
5	Accident Control	Zero "0"	Nos	1	0	1	0	0	0

Difference between KRA & KPI

Sr. No	Performance Scale	Example
1	KRA	1-Actual Performance Nos. /Percentages 2-Organization, Goals/objective Defined 3-Freeze at starting of Business year 4-Evaluation based on monthly Basis 5-Directly Linked with Organization objective (e.g. Production, Quality, Cost, Delivery, Safety, Morale – PQCDSM).
2	KPI	1-Performance Indicators 2-Measured after KRA Score defined 3-KPI helps us to focus on KRA achieved 4-KPI is generally a break up of KRA's 5-KPI cannot be modified and changed unless change in KRA occurred.

Example - KRA & KPI

S. No	KRA	KPI
1	Zero Accident	**KPI**
		1-No of Training hours imparted on Safety (Target Vs Actual)
		2-Adherance to the use of PPE'S (% of employees using PPE's at shop floor)
		3-Housekeeping score (Desired Vs Actual) 4-Safety committee meetings & MOM circulation, communication on notice board (Number of meetings planned Vs Number of meetings held & communication circulated)

Chapter 6 - KRA Vs Annual Increment

Objective-To provide insight to management for Annual increment budget, recognizing consistent performers/business drivers

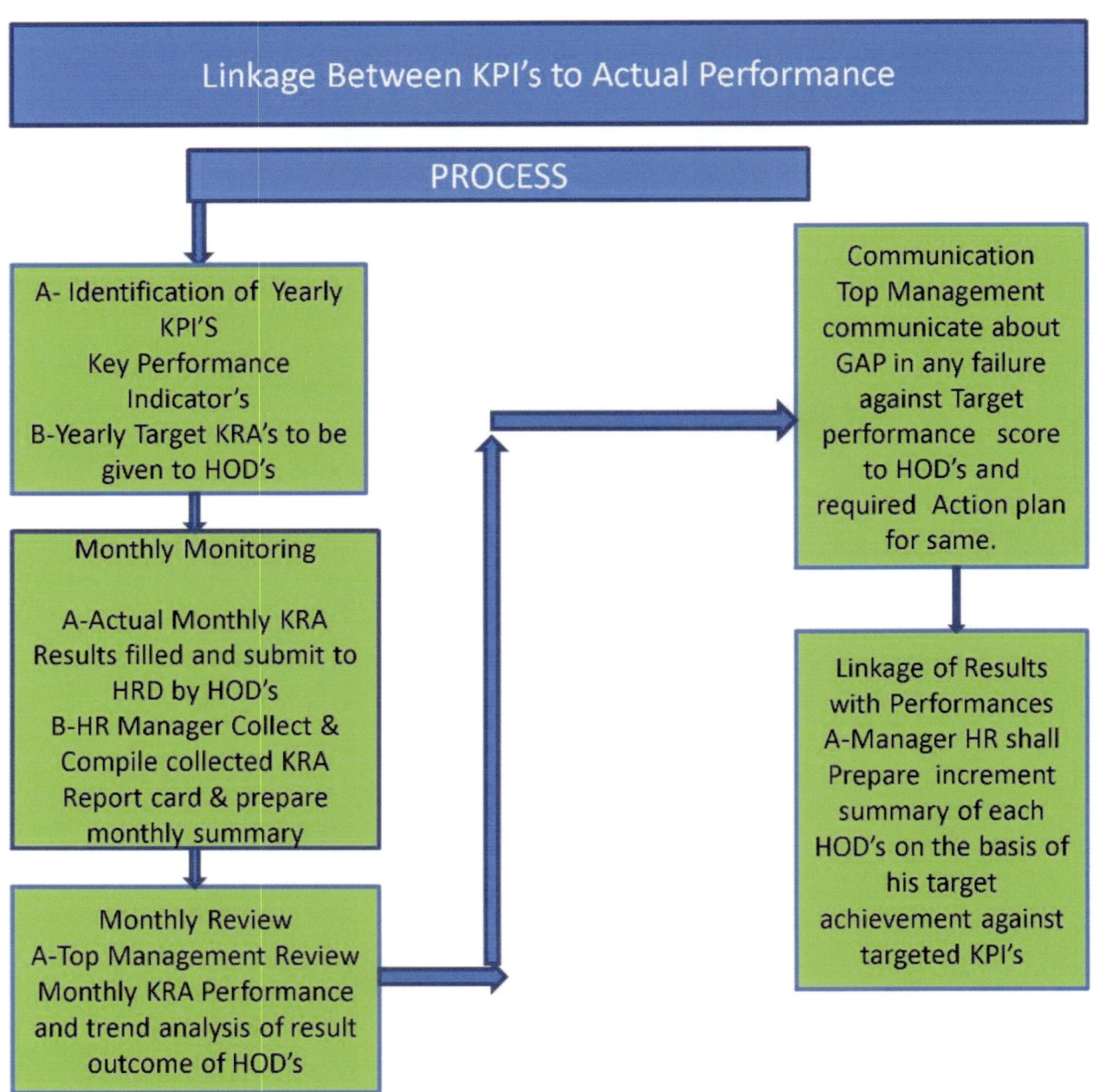

Linkage Between KPI's to Actual Performance(Examples-HR KPI's)

Sample HR Yerarly KPI'S

S.No	KRA'S	Targ.	Apr'15	May '15	Jun'15	Jul '15	Aug'15
1	Increasing Training Mandays	2Hrs/PM/PE	2	2.1	2.1	2.7	2.4
2	Suggestions	280	118	128	155	120	110
3	3's Improvement	75%	65	62	63	62	60
4	KRA Implementation	100%	80	80	80	80	80
5	Zero Accident	0	0	0	0	0	0

Eg. 20% increment on 60000 salary = 12000/- or 1000/- pm

S.No	KRA'S	Targ.	Apr'15	May'15	Jun'15	Jul'15	Aug'15	Positive Trend	Negative Trend	Avg Trend
1	Increasing Training Mandays	2Hrs/PM/PE	2	2.1	2.1	2.7	2.4	+		+
2	Suggestions	280	118	128	155	120	110		-	-
3	3's Improvement	75%	65	62	63	62	60		-	-
4	KRA Implementation	100%	80	80	80	80	80		-	-
5	Zero Accident	0	0	0	0	0	0	+		+
Total								2/5=40%	3/5=60%	2/5=40%

Increment Summary

S.No	Month	KRA's	Postive trend	Negative Trend	Avg Perfromance % (No of +ve trend /No of total trend)	Target Monthly Increment	Actual Monthly Earned Increment
1	Apr-15	5	2	3	40	1000	400
2	May-15	5	2	3	40	1000	400
3	Jun-15	5	2	3	40	1000	400
4	Jul-15	5	2	3	40	1000	400
5	Aug-15	5	2	3	40	1000	400
	Total				40%	5000	2000

Chapter 7 – Control on Absenteeism - Focus on contractual manpower

Objective-To ensure availability of required manpower as per Production Schedule & reduces time on managing manpower

Attendance Improvement Mechanism -Month- Oct-21

Sr. No.	Name	1	2	3	4	5	6	7	8	9	10
1	Ram	Green	Green	Green	Green	Green	Green	Green	Green	Green	Green
2	Shyam	Green	Green	Green	Red	Green	Red	Green	Red	Green	Red
3	Sonu	Green	Green	Red	Green	Green	Red	Green	Green	Green	Green
4	Sanjay	Green	Green	Green	Green	Green	Green	Green	Green	Red	Red

S.NO	Problems	Benifts of Implementing System
1	Difficult for Production Incharge to Complete Productions Numbers	Easy To Complete Shiftwise Target Manpower Vs Actual Achive Targate Production.
2	Difficult for Production Incharge to Complete Productions Numbers in Required Quality	Required Quality Product Will be Produced Regulary, when same employee attending his job on daily basis
3	Time Loss on Arranging New Manpower	No time Loss Occurred for Manpower Arrangement
4	Accident Chances of New Manpower hired (or managed) Immediately working on Machines	Minimising Accident Chances
5	Time Loss on Training New Manpower	No time Loss Occurred for training new
	Legends	Instructions
	Green — Present	1-Fill Green Colour infront of present Employees
	Red — Absent	2-Fill Red Colour infront of Absent Employees

Availability of manpower is one of the main target of an HR professional to start a day on a good note in line with production achievement Vs target.

To understand root causes of absenteeism, an HR professional should be in constant touch with the employees through personal interaction, calls, physical verification in the company (Which is practically challenging).

In order to control absenteeism conventional methods used are leave monitoring, gathering information and daily attendance display on notice boards maintained at shop floor (As mentioned above).

The display of daily attendance supports production department, time office and operators too to identify absentee's attendance on one page. At the beginning of each shift these details helps supervisor to plan the schedule of activities to achieve the target in efficient manner.

This report also help supervisor to take action on habitual absentee's and further provide information to the HR department to take action.

Chapter 8 - Attrition Control - Focus on contractual manpower

Objective-To control Attrition by way of improving facilities, services at workplace to reduce recruitment and cost of retention

Mechanism to improve attrition, attendance, morale & overall performance

Following are some points for attrition control							
Sr No	**Activity**	**Impact**	**Responsibility**	**Sr No**	**Activity**	**Impact**	**Responsibility**
1	Timely Salary distribution	Stability level	HRD	1	Ensure good aptitude	Increase in stable workforce	Contractor
2	First Aid Service	Safe environment practices	HRD	2	Ensure deployment of minimum 12th pass workman	Increase in minimum skill level	Contractor
3	Consistent supply of clean drinking water	Healthy and hygienic work environment	HRD	3	Minimum 95 % attendance	Increase in man-days required	Contractor
4	Availability of fresh, nutritious meal, tea & snacks	Healthy and hygienic work environment	HRD	4	Leave management – Maximum 15 days/Yr	Increase in availability of skilled workman	Contractor
5	Adequate arrangement of Light & Fan at work place	Healthy and hygienic work environment	HRD	5	Leave Management – Ensure minimum workman avail leave at same time	Maintaining balance	Contractor

6	Availability of water and Soap at washroom	Increase in Healthy and hygienic work environment	HRD	6	Deploy disciplined workman who accept mistake and improve on	Increase in morale	Contractor
7	Ensure cleanliness at washroom	Healthy and hygienic work environment	HRD	7	Ensure Workman should use PPE's & should not bring banned items inside the premise eg. Tobacco, bidi etc	Increase in availability of diligent workforce	Contractor
8	Effective grievance redressal system to address A-Overtime, B-Mispunch, C-Salary Calculation, D-Advance	Create environment of openness, trust & care	HRD	8	Ensure to supply required manpower during critical days (Holi, Diwali, etc.)	Ensure business continuity	Contractor
9	Regular training sessions to be conducted	Create healthy environment of learning & growth	HRD	9	Contractor should ensure timely replacement of workers	Decrease in loss of man-hour	Contractor
10	Effective Preventive Maintenance system	Increase ownership	HRD				

11	Good housekeeping & provide dustbin at appropriate places	Healthy and hygienic work environment	HRD				
12	Punching card to be provided to ensue timely recording of attendance resulted in no loss of pay	Increase in satisfaction level	HRD				
13	Reward and recognition	Increase in motivation level resulted in increase in productivity	HRD				

Attrition of employee's at any level is not good for companies growth and business continuity, as resource movement directly impact on day to day working and uncertainty on skill of new joiner's performance is a challenge.

One section of the book address frequent movement of contract workman and how to minimize and control it. Thus, it aims to control the frequent movement of contract workman and impact on production.

Communication, basic amenities, compensation, grievance handling are factors which require monitoring and improvement by the HR professional to curtail the frequent movement of contract workman.

Similarly, to control contractor's performance on deployment of contract workman in terms of timings, discipline, and compensation is the main role failing which frequent movement of contract workman happens.

Chapter 9 - Approaches - To ensure effective Industrial Relations

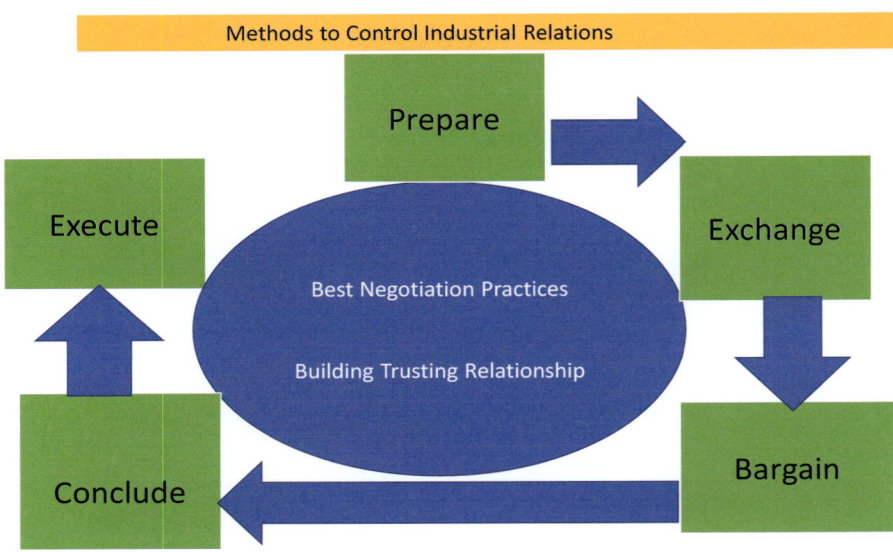

Objective-To develop healthy and effective relations between Employee and Employer to Achieving the Business Objectives.

Preventive & Corrective Action to Control IR

Sr. No	Root Causes	Corrective Actions
1	1-Less & Late Salary & Overtime	Organizing HR Help desk to collect grievances to minimize salary & wages related issues
2	1-Absence of Drinking Water Facility 2-Non Maintenance of available drinking water facility(Water Coolers, Water Taps, Supply of water etc)	Monthly HR Audit to be conducted and audit Score to be included in MRM to improve the Facility
3	1-Insufficient light facility at working stations, Machines etc	Monthly Safety Audit to be conducted and audit Score to be included in MRM to improve the Facility
4	1-Insufficient Fans & Exhaust fans creates berating & health related issues	Monthly Safety Audit to be conducted and audit Score to be included in MRM to improve the facility
5	1-Providing uniform and other facilities provided by other industries	Proposal by HR Manger to be made & presented to Management to increase the facilities

6	1-Unhygienic food provided during lunch and tea brakes 2-Poor Cleaning at canteen results in increasing diseases	Monthly HR Audit to be conducted and audit Score to be included in MRM to improve the facility
7	1-Poor Condition of toilets (Cleanliness, wash basin, absence of soap, exhaust etc)	Monthly HR Audit to be conducted and audit Score to be included in MRM to improve the facility
8	1-Unavailability of transport facility when distance of company and residence of workman is more. 2-Poor Condition of Available Transport facility	Proposal by HR Manger to be made & presented to Management to start Uniform Facility
9	1-Policy related to Reward & Recognition Is Available in papers only, not applicable in reality	Proper implementation of the function & increase Workers involvement for improvement
10	Poor Management thought regarding Workers Participation In Management	Recommendation to management to improve thought process it includes benefits of such groups in line to increase productivity of company(Quality Circle, Kaizen Team)

To ensure harmonious relations with all stakeholders, practicing HR professionals should work on such issues in order to avoid unrest, stoppage of work, grievance on account of non- availability or poor quality of available facilities resource etc. Let us understand how a HR professional can focus and overcome these small but critical issues.

A small but critical issue is the marking attendance, punch machine facility shall be placed at a conspicuous place , looking at the ease of punch. Another major grievance is mis-punch, if an employees misses the punch, uncertainty of getting it corrected , create a grievance till it gets resolved. Imagine a situation where employee is aware of the SOP, he will follow it without creating a negative thought and will remain productive during the shift. Similarly, provision of basic facilities such as clean drinking water, hygienic food, clean urinals, clean shop floor, sufficient light at work stations can be taken care and monitored at regular interval as per the pre determined schedule and maintained as required, else these small grievances, if sustained may leads to less or no production, aggressive behavior of workers, non-cooperation. To conclude all these grievances customer friendly SOP's needs to be in place and followed , a HR professional must ensure that SOP's must be followed to ensure a harmonious environment at the work place.

Chapter - 10 Approach to Control Accidents

Objective-To ensure safe working practices, proactive safe work behavior of employees to achieve ZERO ACCIDENT

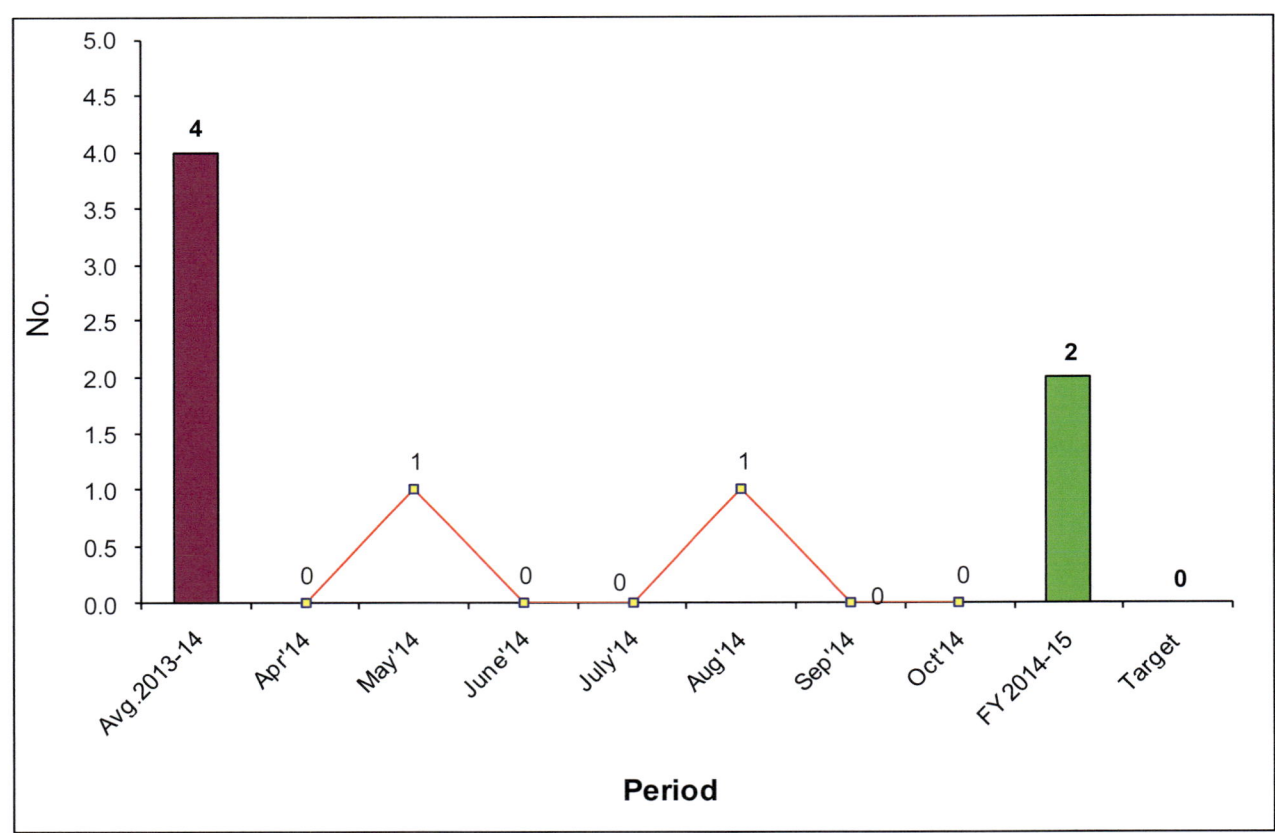

Safe working is essential in every organisation to avoid near misses, miss happenings, loss of man-hours and most importantly prevent injury by providing training before joining and then on the job, refresher safety training sessions also to co-ordinated at regular interval, record of all participants also required to be captured and records

are to be maintained. Besides this visuals and slogans pertaining to safety are also needs to be displayed at conspicuous places in the plant and at work stations.

Following activates are recommended to be followed to ensure Zero Accident

Sr No	Activity	Objective	Frequency	Verification of Actions	Participants or Area to Be Covered
1	Safety Audit	To understand Unsafe Situations, Unsafe Practices and Unsafe Acts	Monthly or Quarterly Depending on indices and analysis of accidents occurred	Monthly HR Report HR MIS	Departments and All Team Members
2	Training	To improve awareness to improve safe working practises and behaviour at workplace	Monthly Every 15 Days	Monthly HR Training Calendar and EHS Audit Report	All Employees
3	Display of Safety Poster, Signage	To inculcate safe practices and eradicate unsafe acts at workplace	Once in year and Replace torn visuals	1-Daily Gemba Meeting 2-Monthly Safety Audit	Entire site
4	Safety Committee Meeting and MOM Circulation	To spread awareness amongst employees and provide Monthly update of meetings	Monthly	Monthly Safety Audit	All Employees
5	PPE'S Adherence	Use of PPE's at workplace to avoid near misses	Daily	Daily Plant Visit	All Employees
6	Administrative Support	To ensure maintenance of civil, electrical and mechanical related issues	Daily	Daily Plant Visit	Entire site

Initiatives to be undertaken to control Unsafe Acts / Practices

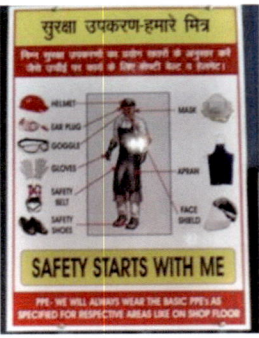 

Educating Safe Working Instruction on Shop Floor

Improvement in 5S & Safe Behaviour

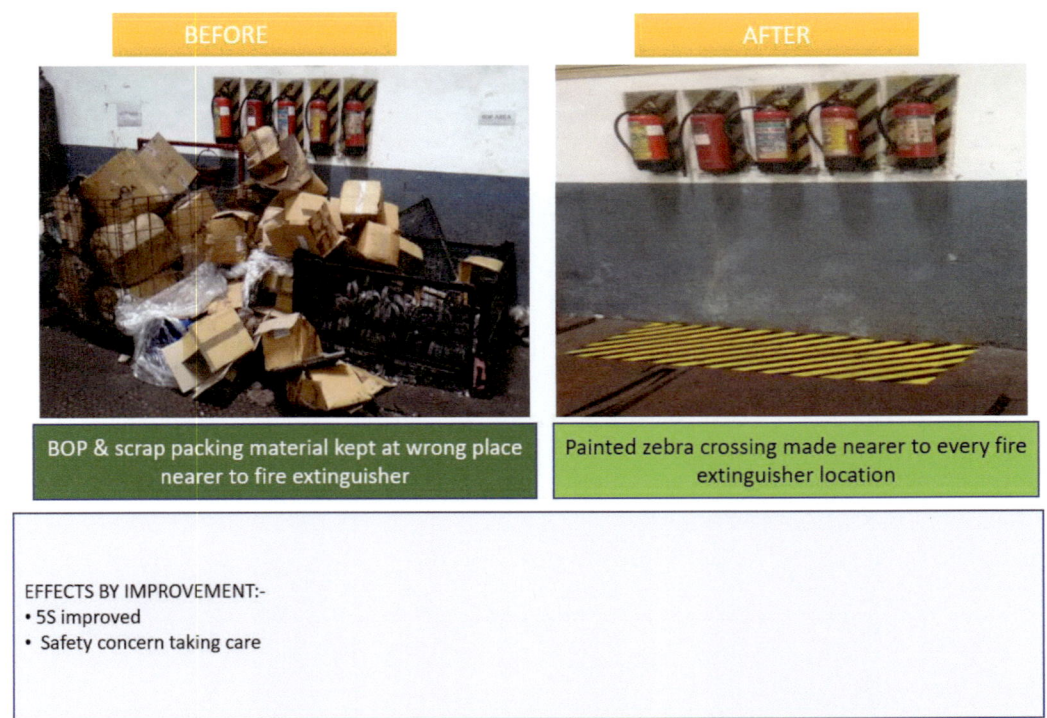

BEFORE	AFTER
BOP & scrap packing material kept at wrong place nearer to fire extinguisher	Painted zebra crossing made nearer to every fire extinguisher location

EFFECTS BY IMPROVEMENT:-
• 5S improved
• Safety concern taking care

Near miss Monitoring - Actions

Near miss monitoring board on shop floor

Monthly near miss summery

CFT meeting on near miss

Actions taken on near miss

Some actions on near miss

Chucker plate in CNC, store gate & dispatch area to avoid accident on account of uneven floor

Iron angle is provided to cover bent iron sheet

Floor repair is done to avoid accident

 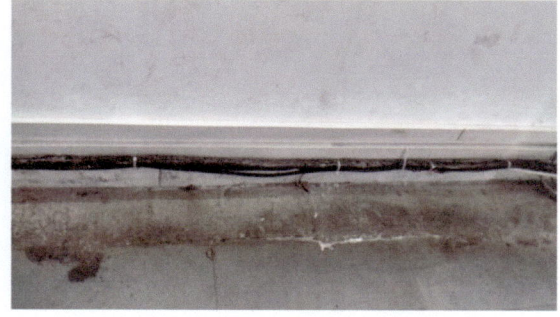

Checker plate repaired at buffing area

Electric wire dressing

23

Fire Fighting – Emergency Response Team (ERT)

Trained Fire Fighters

Sr No	Name	Department	Intercom	Cell No
1	Ajay Kumar	CNC	3421	9988443500
2	Sanjay Sharma	Stores	3455	9979897404
3	Pramod Singh	Maintenance	3422	8888815032
4	Kapil Kumar	Melting	3467	7767087654

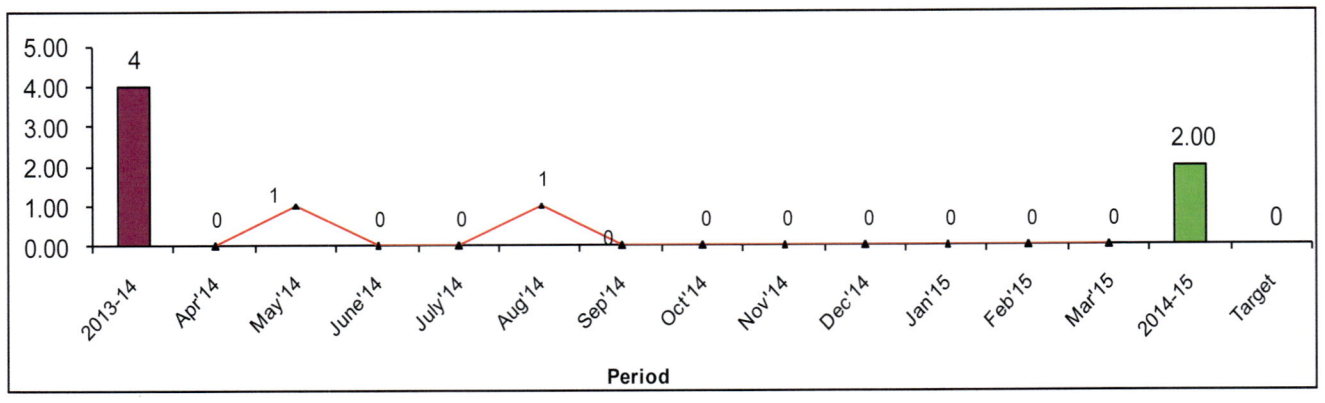

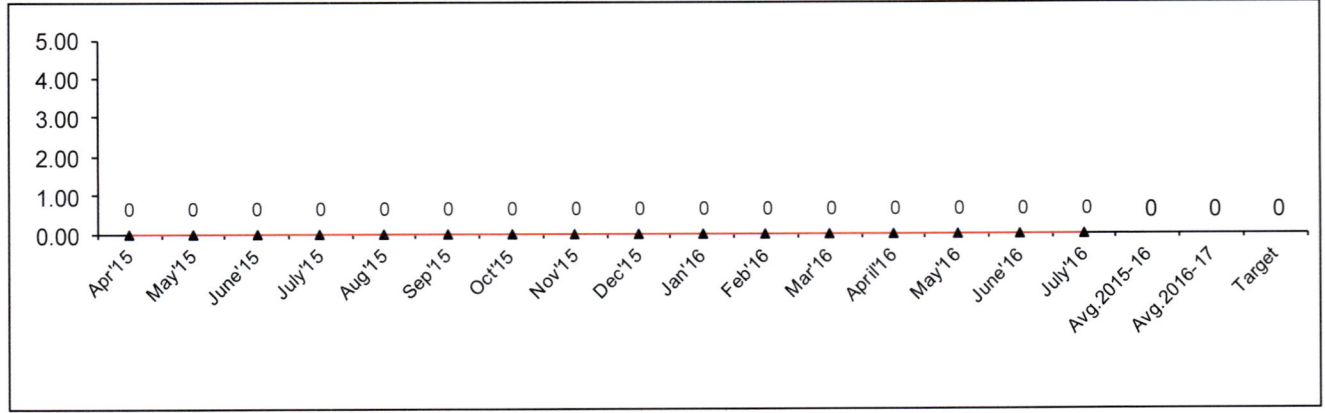

Chapter 11 – Observance Technique - Night Duty Officer

Objective- To ensure smooth operations and ensure discipline

To ensure smooth operations for achieving targets during night shift in a manufacturing plant, organizations follow the practice of deploying NDO to ensure effective co-ordination between departments during the night shift and to keep observations on Environment , Safety , Security and disciplinary issues during night. The night duty officer visits all the plants and observe Unsafe acts, indiscipline and co-ordinate emergency situation if any. Night Duty Officer is expected to ensure the following checkpoints;

Night Duty Officer Report

Date: 13/12/2021

Name – Rahul Kumar   **Designation:**   Sr. Manager

Company Employees – Executive – 15 Workman - 34

Contractual Manpower –

Ramesh Enterprises – 6 – Plant-1

YCS Facility – 10 (Plant – 2 – 5 , ETP- 2, Boiler -3)

OHC – 1

Sr. No.	Place Visited	Contact Person	Observation
1	Plant -1		Normal operations
2	Plant – 2		Normal Operations
3	Boiler/Utility		Normal Operations 2 Coal vehicle is unloaded in night.
4	ETP		ETP is running
5	Safety		Alert
6	Workshop		Normal operations
7	Stores		Close
8	Security		Alert
9	Boundary wall		No issue
10	Plant personnel alertness		Alert
11	Quality of illumination in work area		Needs to improve illumination level at gate entrance. Also front pathway of admin block. Poor illumination in Boiler area and coal storage area.

12	Safety procedure adherence by safety personnel & contract workers Helmet/ Shoes / PPEs		Observed usage of PPE's by all employees. But the issue is that used PPE's are lying on floor in scattered manner at so many places at site.
13	QC lab		Close
14	Environment related issues		Normal
16	OHC		Male nurse found sleeping in OHC.
17	Any significant abnormality		➢ Empty & full Oxygen cylinders are not chained /clamped at Plant-1. ➢ Hazardous Waste container doors were found open. ➢ PPE's are lying on the piping header and on equipments. ➢ Used drums are lying near DG Housekeeping near DG area is poor. ➢ Coal storage area is totally blocked. In case of emergency, difficult to move in that area.

Chapter 12 - Company Vehicle

Objective – To rationalize use of company vehicle during night shift

In general company vehicle is not used during night shifts except emergency situations. Few examles are narrated below

A- In case of accident where injured is referred to the hospital.
B- Material supply – Urgent customer requirement company vehicle can be used after approval of NDO.
C- Transporting an employee in case of break down after approval of NDO.

Chapter 13 – Road Map – Improvement in HR Activities

Objective- Design and develop HR Activities

Human resource is the most important resource for achieving objectives of organization . In order to ensure the effectiveness of the human resource basic factors are to recognize human resource, create strategies to identify skills and knowledge in line with business objective to achieve the short term and long-term business Goals. A road map is a detailed plan with mission, vision, objectives, planned activities, sub activities alongwith monitoring and review mechanism in a way where organization and individual achieve pre determined goals within the deadlines.

Every organization has peculiar challenges, resource and strategies to achieve its goals and targets. In order to achieve Goals and results appended below are the activities to be included in road map of HR department -

A-Effective hiring strategy

B-Induction

C-Skill Development

D-Establishing fair and transparent appraisal systems.

E-Employee Motivation

F-Hassel free Admin Service Services

G-Ensuring healthy and safe work environment

H-Attrition Control

Road Map Format

	Step-1	Step-2	Step-3	Step-4	Step-5	
Sr. No	Vision	Objective	Steps - Implementation	Format	Evaluation	Target Date
1	**Skill development**	1-To upgrade knowledge, Skills & Competencies. 2-To meet Customers satisfaction	1-Identification of Training needs	TNI	% - training sessions Vs Achieved	
			2-Compilation of training needs	Training Classification	% - training sessions	
			3-Annual Training Plan	ATP	% - new projects identified, decline in defects, rejection, attrition, accidents etc.	
			4-Monthly Training Plan	MTP	% - business objectives achieved	
			5-Conduct Month wise Training - Measuring effectiveness & update individual training record	Training Test paper	% - Tests conducted	
2-	**Improvement in overall Plant Visual Display.**	1-Eliminate Waste, Unused material. 2-Establishing best visual display.	Identify Zones, Zones Leaders, Team Members	5's Project Guideline	Adherence to 5S guidelines	
			1-Conduct 5'S Training	Training Attendance Sheet	Identification of unused inventory, products, tools etc.	
			2-Audit 1's & 2s	5'S Audit Sheet.	% - increase in unused space at department	
			3-MIS - 5's Gap	5's Audit Report	Accidents data	

3-	**Reduce Accidents**	1-Creating safe and healthy work environment 2-Ensure "Zero Accidents"	1-Conduct EHS (ISO 14001 & OHSAS 18001) trainings.	Training Attendance Sheet	% - Increase in Awareness wrt safe working habits	
			2-Assess PPE requirements & Ensure Availability of PPE's & uses	PPE requirement Sheet	Increase in no of near misses received and action on it	
			3-Establishing good practices wrt Environment , Health and Safety by conducting meetings, Circulars and Periodic Reviews.	EHS Record File.	Reduction in Accidents, First Aid Cases and near misses. Reduction in leaves on account of health reasons	
			4-Periodic Health Checkup			
4-	**Motivate & Retain Manpower (Reduction In Employee Turnover Rate)**	1-Retaining Motivated & dedicated Manpower.	1-Initiate Motivation Activities.	Activities in place to increase motivation level	% - Attrition	
			2-Conduct Employee Satisfaction Survey.	Employee Satisfaction Survey.	% - Increase in satisfaction level	
			3-Prepare Employee Retention Policy.	Employee Retention policy.	% - Reduction in cost of rehiring and retraining	
5-	**Performance Management**	1-Setting Business Objective Setting 2-Comparing Results wrt defined Objectives.	1-Coordinate in KRA's finalization of Department Heads	KRA, Gap analysis, Action Plan.	% - Business Objective defined	
			2-Cascade KRA"s to team members		Results Comparison Vs set objective	
			3-Collection of Filled KRA's Forms		Action taken on achieved gap against target	

			4-Coordinate with Management Representative regarding Gap in target vs actual results of KRA's.		Compare results and rework on unaddressed objectives	
			5- Prepare plant performance summary report and action plan.			
6-	**Recruitment & Selection**	To keep updated vacant positions & Update Management on positions vacancy	Prepare Updated Recruitment Summary	Monthly Recruitment Report	1-Ensure availability of desired Vs available skills & competencies	
			Update Manpower Requisition form (Replacement and new vacancy)	Manpower requirement summary	Screening of profiles	
		To keep check on vacant positions	1-Sourcing applicants 2-Sourcing Companies 3-Coordination of interviews, and selection of best candidate. 4- Release offer 5-Ensure joining	Assessment Form	Shortlisting of profiles	
		Minimize the time spend on filling vacancy.			Interview, Selection and verification of Candidate	
		To Ensure cost effective & Quality Recruitment.				
7-	**Administrativ e Support**	To provide effective Hygienic work environment.	Prepare & Updated Housekeeping Check sheet.	Monthly Administratio n Check sheet.	Esnure safe, hygienic work environment	
			Prepare & Updated Canteen Check sheet.			
			Prepare list of maintenance of, work station, Canteen, wash room etc			
		To ensure effective Security and administratio	Impart training to Security team	Quarterly Security Performance Review		

			n			
8	**Employee Motivation**	To initiate value & culture building activities	1-Initiate Weekly HR help Desk to resolve employees issues 2-Ensure effective housekeeping 3-Ensure adequate Canteen Services by displaying weekly Menu & supply of nutritious food 4-Sending Birthday/Anniversary wishes to employees 5-Display snaps of Kaizen Hero 6-Display snap of Best Zone Leaders 7-Reward Best employees for different activities.	1-No of issues resolved wrt issues raised 2-Reduction cases indiscipline, absenteeism etc.	1-increase in participation of employees 2-Improvement in motivation index. 3—Increase in ownership	
9	**New Employee induction**	Induction	1-Releasing communication 2-Induction plan 3-Meeting with HO's 4-Receive Feedback from new employee	1-Induction form 2-Quarterly Summary, points discussed and action on points shared by new employee during induction	Hand holding of new employee during induction and during first 3 months	

Chapter 14 - Organization Health Diagnosis and Improvement

Objective-To provide report to the management regarding Organization's strengths, weaknesses, opportunities, threats for preparing strategy

This report based on following points:

1-Training, clarifying objective of training and report submission

3-Follow up with team for data and report submission

3-Data and report collection of participants who attended this training or Process Owners, HOD;s

4-Verifying data and report on the basis of the following:

4.1-Company's monthly department wise report MRM,

4.2-Managers or HOD's Monthly or Quarterly Performance (KRA's Report)

4.3-Internal Rejection

4.4-Customers Returns

4.5-Non- conformance reports by Certification Bodies

4.6 Daily production Report and Rejection and Defects Analysis

Sr No	Activity	Sub Activity	Output Format	Coverage
1	Employee Help Desk	Organise HR Help desk to resolve grievances	1. Summary of grievances 2. Action plan to resolve the grievance	All employees
2	Employee Satisfaction Survey	To collect the points to derive an action plan to improve employee satisfaction	1. Survey report 2. Action plan	All employees
3	Health Diagnosis	Collection of data regarding Production, Maintenance, Quality issues and preparing improvement plan	1. Summary of data 2. Improvement plan	HOD's

Pressure Die Casting -Problem Diagnosis and Solution Summary

Sr. No	Issue	Root Cause	Corrective Action	Resource required	Output	Support Team Required	RE-MARKS
1	Plunger jam	Bad Sleeve condition	Maintain minimum-maximum level with through quality check	Shot sleeve	300 shots /day	Purchase	
2	Casting stuck and broken	Die temperature not controlled due to manual die coat spray	Auto spray to be used	Auto spray and cassette.	480 shots/day	Die Maintenance, Purchase	
3	Die flashing	Blue matching, stain gauge of machine	Die maintenance, proper diagnosis of machine	Elongation, 1 time machine reconditioning	350 shots/day	Die Maintenance and mechanical maintenance	
4	Sprue bush cooling malfunctioning	Nipple and hose pipe not available. Sprue bush hole mismatch	Nipple and hose pipe to be arranged as per requirement.	1/4 MS pipe and rubber hose pipe.	200 shots/day	Die Maintenance	
5	Dent	PDC operation table and fettling table having hard surface.	Wooden block fitment on PDC table and rubber mat for fettling table	Wooden block and rubber mat.	150 pcs save at PDU due to dent	Purchase	

6	High Hydraulic oil temperature	Internal leakage and malfunction of heat exchanger	Valve and heat exchanger to be changed.	Valve and heat exchanger	300 shots /day	Purchase and Maintenance
7	Low Hydraulic oil level in all machines.	Leakage of Hydraulic oil in machines.	Leakage to be arrested	As per requirement by PDC and maintenance	20 shots / day	Maintenance
8	Excess time in die loading.	Non Availability of Spare , I bolt, T bolt, Hydraulic nipple, nut, clamp etc	Spare parts to be provided	As per requirement by PDC	250 shots /day	Purchase
9	Excess time in die repairing during production	Die spare not available as per requirement	Spare to be arranged as requirement	Spare parts of die	50 shots /day	Die maintenance, Purchase
Total shot increase / day					1950	

Store - Problem Diagnosis and Solution Summary

Sr. No	Root Cause	Corrective Action	Resource required	Output	Support Team Required	Remarks
1	Casting packing in worst condition	Casting packing standard should be standardized from vendor end to improve the 5's & inventory Accuracy.	Plastic bin/Corrugated box	To prevent material from dent/scratch & proper accountability.	Marketing / PPC	

2	Space availability	Space to be made available for keeping the materials safe.	Casting storage area required for safe keeping of material	Materials to be prevented from oxidation and direct sunlight.	Management	
3	Not availability of covered area for incoming materials.	Covered area to be provided to store incoming materials.	Covered space	Materials to be prevented from oxidation and direct sunlight.	Management	
4	Quality area for incoming material	IQC area to be defined for inspection of the materials.	IQC Zone to be identified.	To provide IQC area for inspection of the incoming materials	IQC	
5	Defined seating place for Stores person	Store office to be provided for proper working & display the departmental objective & visuals	Suitable Store Office	Efficiency & accuracy will be improved	Management	
6	Ineffective Storage of material	Shade or Roof to be changed for keeping the materials safe.	Change roof	Materials will be saved from rain & proper housekeeping will be maintained	Management	

CNC - Problem Diagnosis and Solution Summary

Sr. No	Root Cause	Corrective Action	Resource required	Output	Support Team Required	Remarks
1	Parts wear out - Tools not replaced	Spare parts to be replaced	Glob dial cam & sector gear assembly	300 parts/day	Maintenance & Purchase	Shaft R (VMC - 113)

2	Axis runout – Dia variation	Spare parts to be replaced	LM guideway & LM block	Reduction in rejection by 50%	Maintenance & Purchase	Shaft R (VMC - 158)
		Spare parts to be repaired	Ball screw of X & Y axis			
3	Chuck de-clamp during power failure - Chuck cylinder & accumulator not working properly	chuck cylinder to be repaired & accumulator to be replaced	Accumulator	Tool cost will be saved	Maintenance & Purchase	FFD Ktea (Turn-104)
4	FRL unit not working - Dia variation	FRL unit to be replaced	FRL unit	Rejection control	Maintenance & Purchase	Export holder (VMC-123)
6	Play in rotary tail stock - Dia Variation	Tail stock to be replaced/repaired	Check at regular interval for replacement	Rejection control & Increase in production	Maintenance & Purchase	RMX & PWC (VMC - 149)
7	Main board malfunction - issue in System booting	Main board to be replaced	New main board	Rejection control & Increase in production	Maintenance & Purchase	For Avtec & Dailmer (Turn-111)
8	Flashing due to wrong	Design to be changed by opting new concept	New tool	Reduction in rejection by 30%	Tool room	Base oil filter casting

tool design - Dimension Variation	

Die Maintenance - Problem Diagnosis and Solution Summary

Sr. No	Root Cause	Corrective Action	Resource required	Output	Support Team Required	Re-marks
1	Heat crack - Hole forming pin broken	Grinding & nit riding hole forming pins to be used	Grinding & nit riding hole forming	25 Shots /day	Purchase	
2	Die temperature is not controlled due to manual die coat spray - Casting stuck and broken	Auto spray to be used	Auto spray and cassette	50 Shots/day	Die Maintenance & Purchase	
3	Blue matching, stain gauge of machine - Die flashing	Die maintenance, Diagnosis of machine	Elongation, one time reconditioning of machines	100 Shots/day	Die Maintenance & Mechanical Maintenance	
4	Non-availability of Cooling assembly nipple & hose pipe - Die cooling	Cooling assembly & hose pipe to be provided	Cooling assembly & hose pipe ID 6mm od 14mm & 1/2"hose clamp	200 Shots/day	Die Maintenance & Purchase	
5	Non availability of die spare (Reed switch, Limit switch, Ejector pins etc.) - Excess time in die repairing	Spare to be arranged	Die spare parts	100 Shots /day	Die Maintenance & Purchase	
Total shot increase / day				475		

Human Resource - Problem Diagnosis and Solution

Sr No	Issue	Solutions	Coverage	Report	Remarks
1	Less And Late Salary	1-Audit before salary processing and action on findings	All Employees	HR Help Desk	
2	Poor Hygiene and Housekeeping	1-Audit at regular interval and action on findings	All Toilets, Drinking Water Facility, Canteen	HR Help Desk	
3	Punch Card and Punching Problem	1-Immediate action to be taken and verification of Action and Problems Solved	All Employees	HR Help Desk	
4	PF & ESI Records to be updated	1-Weekly audit, data to be corrected and updated in order to ensure availability statutory benefits	All Employees	HR Help Desk	
5	Knowledge on Company and Government Welfare Schemes	Training at regular interval to be organized to create Awareness	All Employees	HR Help Desk	
6	Untrained employees	Monthly training and measuring effectiveness	All Employees	Employees Satisfaction Survey Report	
7	Knowledge on Company policy	Monthly training	All Employees	Employees Satisfaction Survey Report	
8	Awareness on Appraisals & KRA	Monthly training to be organized to create Awareness	All Employees	Employees Satisfaction Survey Report	
9	Unsafe working conditions	1-Monthly Safety Audit to be conducted and report to be shared with all employees 2-Actions to be initiated to close on Audit points 3-On the Job and Class Room Training to be Conducted to increase level of awareness	All Employees	Employees Satisfaction Survey Report	
10	Awareness on carrier planning	Carrier Planning Policy to Be Framed and Implemented	All Employees	Employees Satisfaction Survey Report	

Every organization is a set of four pillars Man, Machine, Material and Methods. Their interrelation, interactions and coordination is the basis of growth in an organisation, higher the involvement of 4 M in the day to day working higher the profits, it results in achievement and sustain, grow and lead the product in the market.

Like our bodies require immediate attention during illness or any such situation, organizations take professional consultant's advice on reports or conduct open house / town hall or brainstorming sessions to understand the concerns of employees and arrive at a amicable solution, this is need of the hour.

Let us understand why an organization required to conduct health diagnosis and why corrective action is needed.

First M is the most critical in survival and success of a organization i.e. Man. To understand behavior, moods, anxiety, fear, performances, actions on the tasks assigned to individual or group at regular interval require Employee satisfaction surveys , helps desk or any exercise such as Thomas profiling to find out the root cause of people's mood, behaviors responses.

The second important aspects is Machine, it is important to understand the characteristics of a machine by individual / group working on the Machine. It gives insights of different types of machines, the infrastructure, ideal performance condition, maintenance, training required to operate , temperature, oil, tools, and mechanical and electrical characteristics.

The third important aspects is Material , indicating the type of raw materials, semi-finished, finished material etc is critical in achieving daily productions resulting target sales.

The fourth aspect is Method , it is important to achieve other three M's i.e. MAN, MACHINE & MATERIAL. Growing organizations invest in educating employees by providing training workshop, display relevant information's to educate and transform that learnings into performances of individuals/groups aiming at achieving targets.

Analysis of the above resulted in taking timely corrective and preventive action on errors, communication or sharing of learnings with the individual/group, providing feedback are few approaches in order to achieve organisations short and long term goals.

Chapter 15 - How to Control Air , Water & Oil Leakage

Objective-To control Air, Water & Oil leakages to achieve daily production

Sr No.	Improvement Area	Reason	Sample - Reasons	Sample - Corrective Action	Responsibility	Target Date
1	Oil Leakage	Man	Operator's negligence	Training and observation	HR Co-coordinator & Department Head	
		Machine	Machine's cleanliness	Frequency of machine cleaning, record of cleaning and audit at regular interval	Department Head & QMS Representative	
		Material	Broken oil lubrication points , iron scrap chip lying over lubrication points	Replacement or repair of old mechanical parts, preventive maintenance, record of incidences and Audit at regular interval	Maintenance Head, Department Head, QMS representative	
		Method	Lack of knowledge	Training and observation, Study of oil filling points, oil flow points in machine, oil leakage points and audit at regular interval	HR Coordinator, Department Head, QMS representative	
2	Water Leakage	Man				
		Machine				
		Material				
		Method				
3	Air Leakage	Man				
		Machine				
		Material				
		Method				

To ensure smooth operations, shop floor and machines on shop floor shall be maintained and resources such as Air, Water and Oil are to be preserved and wastage to be controlled in order to achieve neat and clean shop floor condition and saving resources for optimum utilization of the resources.

Let us start with Air. Air gun, air compressor and all such air pressure point to be monitored at regular interval and maintained in order to arrest air wastages, availability and optimum use are the targets of an organization beside taking control on wastage of such resources which directly impact on consumption of the resource.

Similarly, oil and water wastage are to be controlled and its optimum utilization to be done.

Oil is flammable too, therefore handling, while filling or leakages may result in fire and accidents beside resource wastage. Similarly, oil storage is to be maintained safely as per SOP in order to prevent accidents

Clean and adequate water supply is also one of the important aspect needs to be maintained, provided and wastage to be stopped.

While working on the table we can understand basic reasons of leakages, impact of leakages and benefits of stopping such leakages. Check sheet to collect data is the first step to observe and analyze the root causes and team meeting on data collected and strong action plan in place to control is the next step.

Note-Water and Air Leakages Columns are blank in format which is learning exercise, like Oil Leakages, employees responsible for Water and oil leakages are expected to fill this reason or supervisor will fill after getting facts, data of these reasons.

Chapter 16 - Customer Satisfaction Improvement Matrix

Objective -To understand value of customer satisfaction (Meeting daily production and supplies delivered at customer's end)

Sr No	Criteria	Unit of measurement	Frequency	Remarks
1	Schedule Production	Actual Production Vs Target	Monthly	
2	Quality	No of OK Production Received against Total Production booked at customer end	Monthly	
3	Timing	Timing of Material Received at customer end against Standard time of delivery of product	Monthly	

4	Adherence to packaging standard	Number of customer complaint received in terms of packaging against standard packaging criteria	Monthly	
5	Customer response time	Actual time taken against required time	Monthly	
6	Audit marks	Total Marks Achieved against total Maximum Marks	As & when required	
7	Customer quality ratings	Position of Company in ranking table of customers	Monthly	
8	Customer delivery rating	Position of Company in ranking table of customers	Monthly	
9	Opportunity for improvement (OFI)	Number of OFI points Converted against number of OFI points given by customers	As & when required	

In today's cut throat competitive times , business is running on daily schedules, higher customer satisfaction , improved customer relation. In the table mentioned above, we have studied the points for improvement mentioned in the table for planning and execution to achieve day to day sales.

In other words, each point written in the table has a value too, by addressing or working on these points, a team can improve and achieve the desired results. Internal inspection is also important for management to address on above subjects on priority for ensuring supplies to customers.

While executing the above , company performance in market will improve and customers will get attracted to do business with the company who work on priority to address the customers issues.

Points taken in this table will also impact directly on each production substations required for supplies, and demand will be understood by team member's and resulted in improvement in the day-to-day working aiming to achieve target sales.

Chapter 17 - Capacity Building

Objective-To provide tools for strengthening organization's objectives in line with current & future objectives

Sr No	Objective or Benefit	Activity	Frequency	Coverage	Category
1	1-Reduction in loss	Suggestion / Kaizen	Monthly	All employees	Worker's participation In Management
	2-Improve employee's participation				
	3-Improve employee's morale				
2	1-Increasesing Awareness of Product/Process	Class Room Training / On The Job Trainings	Monthly	All employee	Capacity Building
	2-Improve Skills/Competencies				
	3-Reduce loss in manufacturing				
	4-Improve Team Work				

3	1-Improvement in Shift production	Performance Appraisal (KRA Review)	Quarterly	All employees	Productivity Improvement
	2-Structured Feedback to minimize Losses on account of	(Review, Feedback & Improvement)			
	A-Production issues				
	B-Process issues				
	C-Decision Making				
	D-Skill Gap				
	E- Normal & Abnormal Losses				
	3-Improvement In increasing Transparent & Competitive Work Culture				
4	1-Improvement in Team Work	Employee Engagement	Monthly	All employees	Capacity Building

Chapter 18 - Production Improvement

Objective - To understand reasons for daily production losses and action to control

Format For Target Vs Actual Production Improvement Analysis

S.No	Machine Name	Operators Name	Target Production	Actual Production	Operators Att.	Standard PM Time	Actual PM Time	Recomded Die Change Over Number/Time

In order to achieve production wrt target production on daily basis, each employee such as Helper, Operator, Supervisor, Engineer, Manager Production, Manager Maintenance are directly responsible for production actives. In their day to day working all employees must ensure their job must be in line with the job assigned / responsibly to achieve shift wise production.

Actual Die Change Over Number/Time	No Of Pieces Rejected	Reason of Rejection	No of Min Machine Idle	Plunger	Tooling	Trolley	Oil	Clothes	Operator Avail.	Pending for decisions

Along with them, system auditor also is equally responsible to conduct scheduled & transparent audits and sharing results of audit to the employees as per the frequency defined . This exercise is helpful to understand daily losses arising on account of various diversified reasons mentioned in the table to collect data and work on the required areas to ensure the improvement in production.

After filling data in the table mentioned above on hourly, daily, weekly, monthly basis, an organization is able to understand the problem area and can take action on repeated or major areas, this also help each individual to learn, understand and improving the performance in line with daily required production.

Chapter 19 - Productivity Improvement

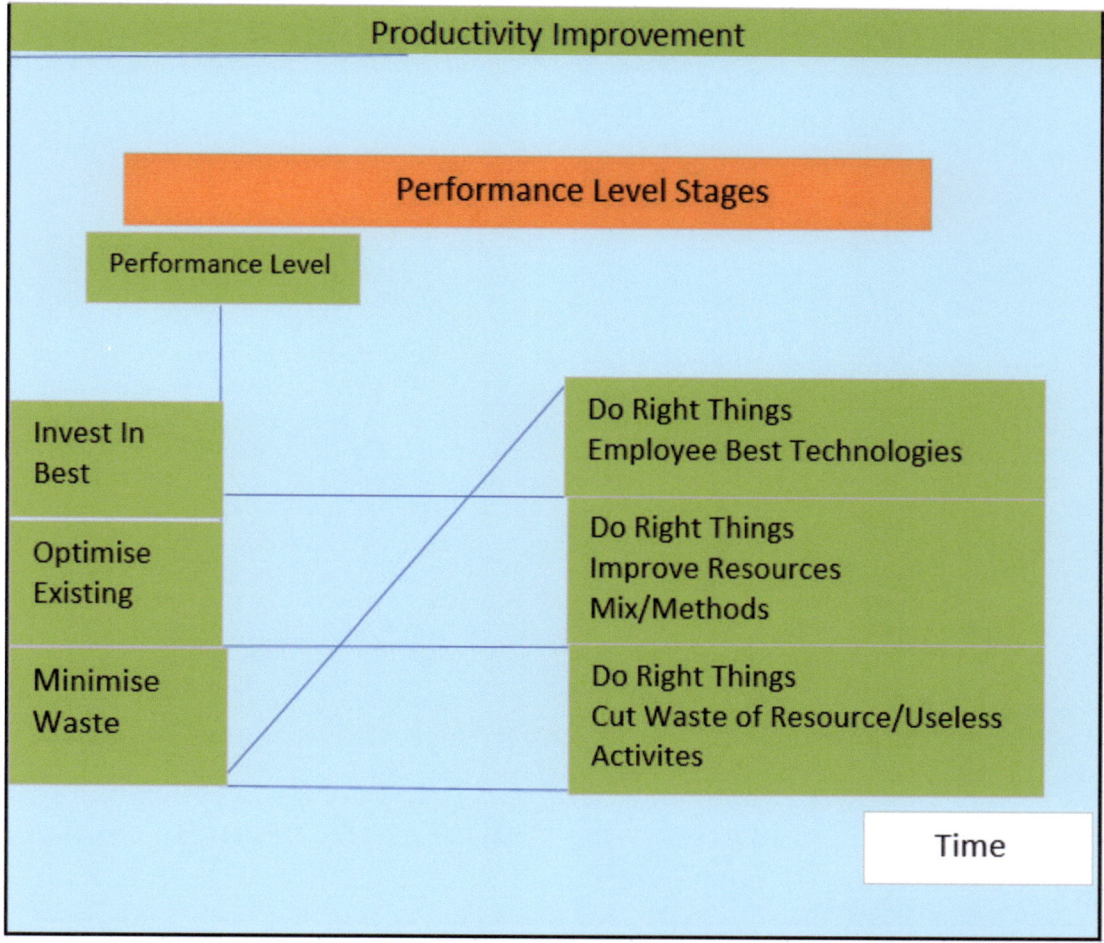

Increasing cost is one of main concern for organizations and to sustain and survive in todays tough competition, cost saving measures are to be adopted to perform at par.

Following are few points, on which a team can work and achieve feasible savings :

1-Production- reduce change over time, increase tool life by better up-keep, support maintenance by cleaning machine, use of other production support materials such as bins, trays, air gun, etc. can convert into efficiency at work.

2-Quality- Reduce rejection % overall or on specific products to support PPC in converting more sales resulted in increase in sales. Increase pokes to ensure minimum mistakes during working.

3-PPC-Save packed material by packing (Tarpaulin or plastic covers- tirpal) to avoid loss due to moisture in rainy season, reduce time in material movements.

4-Store- Control effective check on consumables, push material stored at the end to their customers for further process to speed up production.

5-Maintenance- Effective preventive maintenance to ensure, occurrence of repeated problems, reduce machines idle time on account of maintenance, minimize oil leakages from machine to convert oil leakage into oil saving , compare alternative electrical instruments (bulb, sockets, fuse etc.) for electricity saving.

6-HRD -Motivate teams by training and better services to enhance the skill level.

Chapter 20 - Employee Engagement

Objective-To understand importance and results achieved by engaged workforce

Employee engagement is an area on which all companies focus to achieve set results, for **business growth** , employee engagement is one of the vital tool , an HR professional can achieve high morale and motivated team by applying the engagement tools.

An organization where development of human capital or engagement through HR tools is not used frequently, the average happiness index is low

A sound employee engagement plan if implemented after pulse / employee satisfaction survey (behavioral, functional) creates wonders for the organization. When engagement activities like, motivation, display of achievement / snaps, Rewards to winners in various internal competitions becomes habit, employees feel rejuvenated, upbeat and that positive energy can be measured in increase in improvement activities, improved happiness index, less leaves on account of illness are few examples to understand psychological shift.

Terminology to understand improvents:

1- Reduction in Attrition

2- Achievement of Business Goals

3- Control on Absenteeism

4- Reduction in Rejection

5- Increase in Suggestions & Kaizen %

6- Increase in Quality Circle Formation

7- High Morale or overall improvement in PQCDSM index.

Employee engagement tool is one of the best tool to improvise employee's performance index in various categories.

Printed by Libri Plureos GmbH in Hamburg,
Germany